Young Freemasons?

Also from Westphalia Press

westphaliapress.org

Young Freemasons?

Frank S. Land's
Order of DeMolay

Introduced and Edited by
Guillermo De Los Reyes

WESTPHALIA PRESS
An imprint of the Policy Studies Organization

Young Freemasons?
Frank S. Land's *Order of DeMolay*

For information:
Westphalia Press
1527 New Hampshire Ave., N.W.
Washington, D.C. 20036

ISBN-13: 978-1935907268
ISBN-10: 1935907263

Cover design by Taillefer Long
at Illuminated Stories:
illuminatedstories.com

Updated material and comments on this
edition can be found at the Westphalia Press
website: westphaliapress.org

For Alain Bauer,
Who knows all the Secrets.

Introduction to the New Edition

Dad Land's Boys

Freemasonry considers the age at which it accepts initiates differently in different countries. While often the minimum age is 21, sometimes it is 18 and recently more grand lodges have been changing from 21 to 19 or 18. A long-standing tradition has been that sons of Freemasons are called Lewises and in a great many jurisdictions can enter at 18.

However, it is also common for lodges to sponsor some sort of youth affiliate. In Mexico, youth associations sponsored by lodges are widespread, often as chapters of Asociacion de Jovenes Esperanza de la Fraternidad (which was founded in Cuba in 1928 and also has chapters in the United States and Latin America). In the United States there still exists a movement known as the Boy Builders, which has declined over the years but which some lodges sponsor. The most well known youth movement associated with Masonry originated as well in the United States but is now found in many countries, the Order of DeMolay.

E

DeMolay was the project of Frank S. Land, a prominent Kansas City businessman who used the legends of the Masonic Knights Templar to create the order. He was careful to avoid any claims that it was a junior sort of Freemasonry, but the order has its secret words and rituals. It is sponsored by individual lodges as well as by grand lodges, and the "dads" or advisers are mostly Freemasons. Since it takes years to rise in its international hierarchy, often the top leaders are already Freemasons of some experience by the time they achieve grand rank. Moreover, a considerable number of the present day Masonic officers in grand lodges have had a connection with DeMolay in their youth.

The following text is of considerable historical interest because it represents a catalogue of Frank Land's still-forming ideas for the order when it was in its beginning stages. Some things that he created have remained remarkably the same and others have fallen by the wayside. Land's ideas were sufficiently attractive to influence other fraternal movements in the founding of their own junior groups both for girls and boys. The Columbian Squires of the Knights of Columbus are a case in point, as are the Pythian Sunshine Girls, Junior Odd Fellows, the Prince Hall Knights of Pythagoras and Circles, and myriad others.

F

DeMolay has its female counterparts that also require adult Masonic advisers, including the Order of the Rainbow and Job's Daughters, as well as the lesser known such as the Eastern Star Constellations and Triangles. Understandably, these groups for girls often pair up with DeMolay chapters for social events. All are ritualistic and have their own collection of symbols that they teach to candidates. Uniting this family of Masonic-related societies and making them different from other youth movements is the emphasis on ceremony and the connections with the adult lodges and chapters.

This is an understudied area of society, and one that raises questions about its effects on those who have been involved. A famous example in which an individual gives DeMolay credit for its influence on him is President Bill Clinton, who was a very active member. In his autobiography *My Life* he says, "I didn't need to belong to a secret fraternity to have secrets" but has lots of good things to say about the order, which he admits was his major extracurricular activity as a youth. In 1995 when Clinton was visiting Manila as President, he insisted on making time in a tight schedule to meet Philippine DeMolay youth in Quirino Stadium. Clearly the order has considerable significance to its members, and this artifact from its beginnings may provide some idea of its import.

G

What makes this pamphlet noteworthy is that it appeared when Land was still sorting out the rituals and traditions of the new fraternity. He borrowed heavily from the Masonic York Rite and especially from the Masonic Knights Templar. So what we have is a premier on organizing, something rather unique in the literature of secret societies. Various rituals and ceremonies are being put forward, some of which fell by the wayside and some of which have persisted.

Given the desire of secret societies to cloak themselves in antiquity, it is not often that one is permitted such a behind the scenes look.

Guillermo De Los Reyes

H

Order of
DeMolay

" I do so Promise
and Vow "

Foreword

To you just entering the portals of DeMolay, a wholehearted welcome is extended by the great legion of its membership. You are now a part of the most select group of young men to be found anywhere in the world. You have been handed the torch of high endeavor and there is a solemn injunction upon you that it must be ever kept burning. Thousands of young men have borne it in the past and millions will bear it in the future. It is an important stewardship whose responsibilities should never be shirked.

More than six hundred years have passed since the unconquerable spirit of Jacques DeMolay blazed forth with a power that dimmed the material flames which consumed his body. It was a spiritual blaze of moral chivalry which you and other young men have inherited from this noble Knight; a chivalry which prompts its members to be clean in all things and always ready to protect and defend the weak, the helpless and the oppressed. Truly a creed you will be proud to exemplify before the world.

If you are a sincere seeker you will find DeMolay of real aid in solving many perplexing problems. Your membership in this Order will profit you according to the measure of service you render its cause. As you give so shall you gain. Its spiritual, mental and physical standards will aid the manliness within you. Its forebearance and brotherly love will be yours to adopt and exemplify.

Frank S. Land

Judge Alexander G. Cochran
Grand Master Councilor
Order of DeMolay

A DeMolay's Ethics

A DeMolay serves God.

A DeMolay honors all womanhood.

A DeMolay loves and honors his parents.

A DeMolay is honest.

A DeMolay is loyal to ideals and friends.

A DeMolay practises honest toil.

A DeMolay's word is as good as his bond.

A DeMolay is courteous.

A DeMolay is at all times a gentleman.

A DeMolay is a patriot in peace as well as war.

A DeMolay is clean in mind and body.

A DeMolay stands unswervingly for the public schools.

A DeMolay always bears the reputation of a good and law-abiding citizen.

A DeMolay by precept and example must preserve the high standards to which he has pledged himself.

Frank S. Land
Grand Scribe and Founder
Order of DeMolay

The Founding of DeMolay

An abiding confidence in the manliness inherent in the youth of all nations was the primary reason Frank S. Land, of Kansas City, Missouri, founded the Order of DeMolay. His experiences had taught him that young men who had courage and ability were the clean living, right-minded fellows who loved their parents, respected their elders, believed in God and exemplified these qualities at all times.

Several years before "Dad" Land started this young men's organization he had enjoyed the friendship and confidence of a fatherless boy, named Louis G. Lower. It was a friendship that grew with the years and one wherein young Lower sought and received much timely advice. He frequently visited Mr. Land's office and ere long was usually accompanied Louis G. Lower by some of his chums. Soon there were nine of these lads making his office a headquarters. Besides counselling with their friend over personal problems, they listened to his tales of famous heroes in history.

One night—March 24, 1919, to be exact—this group of young fellows had gathered as usual, when suddenly "Dad" Land asked them how they would like to form a club. The idea was enthusiastically received and no time was lost in organizing.

When it came time to select a name, the nine were a unit in favor of the name of DeMolay Council, after Jacques DeMolay, a famous Frenchman who had shown marvelous courage in times of stress.

The first fellow to be made a member of this new organization was young Lower. Therefore he was the first DeMolay in the world. The eight other young men who formed that foundation group of DeMolay, were: Gorman A. McBride, Jerome Jacobson, William Steinhilber, Elmer Dorsey, Ivan Bentley, Clyde Stream, Ralph Sewell and Edmund Marshall.

These young men constituted the start of Kansas City Chapter, "Mother Chapter of the World."

Frank A. Marshall
Author of the Ritual
Order of DeMolay.

Precepts and Ritual

The seven cardinal virtues, or precepts, of DeMolay are Love of Parents, Reverence, Patriotism, Cleanness, Courtesy, Comradeship and Fidelity. Truly a powerful array of the qualifications that make for real manhood.

Around these precepts the impressive DeMolay ritual was written by Frank A. Marshall, a newspaper editor, long prominent in Masonic activities.

Growth of DeMolay

The second meeting of DeMolay was held April 1, 1919. It was attended by the original nine members and twenty-two of their friends. A total of thirty-one young men pledged to clean living. This gathering has since become recognized as the charter meeting.

The First Forty-seven Members.

Sessions were held weekly and at each new members were admitted. The hundred mark was reached, then the two hundred, and so on until the membership had reached huge proportions. In November, 1919, the name of the organization was changed from DeMolay Council to the Order of DeMolay. New chapters were springing up in communities outside of Kansas City and DeMolay was started on the highway of accomplishment which is making it worldwide in scope and power. On January 1, 1926, it was estimated that nearly a quarter of a million young men had knelt at its altar.

Chapter Organization Plan of DeMolay

Each DeMolay chapter must be sponsored by a recognized Masonic body or an organization composed exclusively of Freemasons.

Each local chapter is under the control of an Advisory Council selected from the membership of the sponsoring body.

A chairman directs the advisory council. Another of its members is appointed advisor of the chapter. He is known as "Dad" and should always be addressed by that title. If desired, the chairman and "Dad" of a chapter may be the same person.

The Grand Council

By March, 1921, the Order of DeMolay had become national and international in its activities necessitating the formation of a governing body. To organize such a body, Freemasons from all parts of the United States met in Kansas City, Missouri, and formed the Grand Council. Its personnel is limited to fifty active members and as many deputies as approved by the Council. Several foreign countries are represented.

Every member of DeMolay, all chapters, advisory councils and sponsoring bodies, insofar as chapters of De-Molay are concerned, yield allegiance to the Grand Council whose See is at Kansas City, in the State of Missouri.

The Grand Council is the supreme authority in all matters appertaining to the government of the whole Order.

The members and the deputies of the Grand Council are the active heads of DeMolay in the jurisdictions assigned to them. Their acts and decrees are absolute, insofar as they do not conflict with the Constitution and Statutes of the Order.

Importance of Advisory Council

A strong factor in the success of a DeMolay chapter is its advisory council. This council is composed of not less than six Freemasons. It is held accountable to the Grand Council for the conduct and government of a chapter. The men who comprise each advisory council give freely of their time and attention to this work because of their interest and faith in young men. They, themselves, derive great pleasure from the associations and friendships thus developed. This is an important matter for you to consider. Your co-operation will be a valued aid to your advisors; your inattention and opposition will woefully retard them in their work.

DeMolay Not a Junior Masonic Fraternity

You should know that the Order of DeMolay is not a junior Masonic fraternity. There can be no such organization. Freemasons aid DeMolays and Masonic bodies sponsor chapters just as they do any other laudible undertaking. DeMolay cannot and does not insure future membership in the Masonic fraternity.

The DeMolay Way

The decorum of DeMolays during chapter meetings should be one of dignity.

A fellow DeMolay should always be addressed as "Brother."

A member of the Masonic fraternity is addressed as "Mr." and you should avoid the liberty of unwarranted use of first names or nicknames when conversing with older men.

Always exchange greetings with a young man who wears a DeMolay emblem or gives other evidence of being a member. He is a brother and needs no formal introduction.

Your chapter is your DeMolay home. Encourage other young men to enter it as members when you find them to possess the desired qualities. Take no person into this home whom you do not consider a fit associate.

Be manly in behavior and general appearance. Do not smoke at the entrance of your meeting place or while in processions. Keep your eyes to the front when on parade. You, your chapter and the Order of DeMolay are being judged by all onlookers.

When prayers are said at a public or private DeMolay gathering, every member must go to his left knee, with bared head, and remain thus until the chaplain has concluded, at which time all in unison should say, "Amen."

Chapter Ethics

Always go to the altar and give the sign when entering or retiring from the chapter room during chapter meetings.

Never pass between the Master Councilor and altar except when participating in degree work.

Do not smoke in the chapter room.

Pay your chapter dues. This is absolutely essential to the well-being of your chapter and of the entire DeMolay organization. Every DeMolay should take pride in keeping himself clear on the books of his Order. At the Grand Council headquarters is a complete record of your DeMolay affiliations. It is an imperishable record. Make it one of which you will be proud.

Dress and Decorations

When attending DeMolay functions and meetings, a member may wear business or dress clothes. This is optional. Coats should be worn except in extreme warm weather.

The membership medallion should be worn suspended from the neck.

Correct Attire.

The official DeMolay pin and guard should be worn over the heart on the vest or shirt. It should never be worn upon the coat. If desired, a small DeMolay button for the coat lapel can be secured at any jewelers.

When buying DeMolay jewelry of which the emblem is a part, look upon the back for the manufacturers' trade mark and the words, "Patented Oct. 25, 1921." Medallions have on the reverse side the serial number and words, "Patented May 19, 1925, Grand Council Order of DeMolay."

These designations are your protection.

Medallions

DeMolay medallions may be obtained from reputable jewelers.

Medallion Service Stripes

A member should have the proper ribbon for his medallion in accordance with the regulations.

A special ribbon is issued with each medallion in accordance with DeMolay regulations. They are as follows:

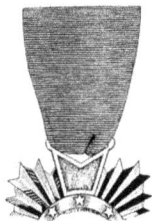

Medallion With Ribbon Denoting Two Years' Service.

Ribbon for Less Than One Year of Service.

All medallion ribbons have a thin white stripe for each year as an active DeMolay.

Active DeMolay, plain blue ribbon.

Active DeMolay who is a Past Master Councilor, blue ribbon with two white stripes running lengthwise.

Active DeMolay during period he is Master Councilor, blue ribbon with one white stripe running lengthwise.

Majority member who holds a majority certificate purple ribbon.

Majority member who is a past Master Councilor, purple ribbon with two white stripes running lengthwise.

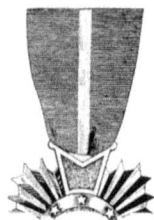

Master Councilor's Ribbon.

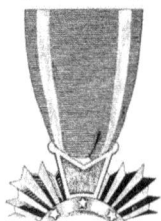

Past Master Councilor's Ribbon.

Majority member who has become a Master Mason, red ribbon.

Majority member who is a past Master Councilor and has become a Master Mason, a red ribbon with two white stripes running lengthwise.

Advisory Council Medallions

The advisor of a chapter wears a gold medallion attached to a ribbon of blue and gold. Other members of the council wear gold medallions attached to a ribbon of white and gold.

DeMolay medallions are of striking design and form a distinctive decoration.

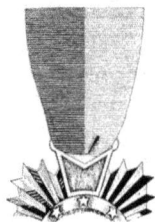

Advisor's Ribbon.

Attendance and Visitation

Show your current dues card to the sentinel of your chapter in order to receive the "word of the day."

When visiting another chapter show your patent and dues card to the sentinel with a request that you be examined. The sentinel will then communicate with the Master Councilor, who will delegate a committee to conduct this examination. When you are found in good standing and worthy, you will be escorted into the chapter room by this committee and formally presented.

 While being examined you will be required to recite both obligations and to give the signs of the Order—all from memory. Before being examined you will take the following oath upon a Bible:

"I.., do hereby sincerely swear that I have received the Initiatory and DeMolay degrees in a legally constituted chapter of the Order of DeMolay; that I am not now a suspended or expelled member, and know of no reason why I should not visit this chapter."

You must not vouch for a visiting DeMolay unless you have sat in open chapter with him. The assurance of his eligibility must be given to the Master Councilor, as well as to the sentinel. An examination is not required in this case.

Status of a Majority Member

In jurisdictions which permit visitation of chapters by former DeMolays, who have reached the age of twenty-one years, you must display your current yearly majority card or majority certificate. These cards and certificates are issued by the Grand Council and, to be acceptable, both must be properly countersigned with your signature.

A majority member cannot vote or hold office in a chapter but, in jurisdictions where permissible, is a welcome guest at meetings should he possess a proper majority card or certificate.

Tell It To "Dad"

When in trouble go at once to your chapter "Dad". He will not humiliate you, but will give you counsel and aid. What you tell him will be kept absolutely confidential. You can trust him.

If you are in a strange or distant town or city and in trouble or distress, get in touch with the chairman or "Dad" of the chapter of that community. You must show him your patent and dues card both properly countersigned. For this reason always have them with you no matter where you go. Should you need financial assistance, the advisor will make a telegraphic appeal to your chapter for funds. *Positively no chapter is required to aid you unless you can show your dues card and patent.*

Grand Master Councilor

The Grand Master Councilor of DeMolay is Judge Alexander G. Cochran, of St. Louis, Missouri. He is a recognized leader in Freemasonry and the Active Member in the State of Missouri for the Supreme Council, Southern Jurisdiction of the United States, A. A. S. R. He is also a member of all York Rite Bodies in his home city. His influence and time, in behalf of the Order of DeMolay, has been a powerful factor in the success of this organization. To know Judge Cochran is to honor, respect and love him.

Founder and Grand Scribe

Practically every great movement or enterprise has been developed around some one person. The Order of DeMolay proves this general rule. It is built around and directly associated, in the minds of all who know about the organization, with Frank S. Land, its founder and Grand Scribe.

Under his guidance, and with the able support of the members and deputies of the Grand Council, heads of departments at the national offices and leaders of chapters everywhere, he has seen the Order become worldwide in scope and membership and recognized as the most powerful of its kind. All this since March, 1919.

Grand Scribe's Headquarters

The Grand Scribe's staff is composed of loyal department heads who are recognized leaders in their particular
fields. These men have been selected by Mr. Land with the
approval of the Grand Council. Each department has
trained workers efficiently carrying out the instructions
given them. However, so well organized is the Grand
Scribe's office that the various departments work as one
big unit.

Ninety-five percent of the total business transacted in
these offices is by mail. During the busy periods from
eight to ten sacks of mail daily are frequently sent out
and received. Also many express packages. Add to this
the vast amount of clerical work necessary to keep a record
of the chapters and membership of DeMolay and you will
readily appreciate what an immense volume of business is
handled.

Less than twenty-five workers including department
heads, do it all.

This is acknowledged to be one of the smallest staffs
in the country transacting the headquarter's affairs of an

Partial View of Grand Council Office.

organization of DeMolay size. It is a remarkable fact that the operating cost of the Grand Council is less than that of any similar movement in the world today.

Charles A. Boyce is General Auditor for the Grand Council and has supervision over the clerical force in the Grand Scribe's offices. Before joining the Grand Scribe's staff, Mr. Boyce was auditor for a big midwestern railroad company. It is due to his careful supervision that the immense volume of DeMolay business is handled by such a small force of workers.

Charles A. Boyce.

The office management is in charge of John C. Egley. A thorough mastery of detail and the ability to arrange the office work so that it is handled in an efficient, direct manner attests Mr. Egley's value to the headquarter's staff.

The Grand Scribe's offices and staff can be likened to the hub of an immense wheel that has spokes reaching to all corners of the world. Problems of local, state, national and international importance are handled. It is continually at work in the service of every DeMolay.

John C. Egly

Office Activities

To detail all of the transactions would require a book in itself. Every phase of the business of the Grand Council is centered here. For instance, there is a card record of every DeMolay in the world and an active file of the thousands of Freemasons who are members of chapter advisory councils. From the Grand Scribe's headquarters are issued all patents, petitions, charters, record books, membership cards, service certificates, majority certificates, pamphlets describing various activities, special information which may be desired, in fact, everything that has any bearing on the Order of DeMolay as a whole.

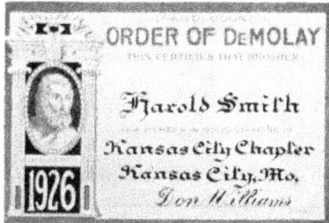

1926 Membership Card.

The big job of the Grand Scribe's staff is the receiving and verifying of annual reports. These reports define the standing of every De-Molay and of every chapter. Each is checked back against the records on file in this office. Any discrepancies found are investigated and adjusted. The magnitude of this work can be visualized when you remember that more than 250,000 members have received the degrees in more than 1,500 chapters in 8 countries.

A visit to these offices is a revelation to all who are interested in DeMolay. In the course of a year members of the Order, chapter advisors and other persons are welcome callers—not only from all sections of the United States, but from foreign countries as well.

Department of Program and Activities

This branch of DeMolay under the Grand Scribe is directed by Roy E. Dickerson. To it he brought twenty years of success in welfare work among young men, for other organizations.

Roy E. Dickerson.

Activities instituted and sponsored by this department include: State Conclaves, Regional and National Camps, Leaders' Conferences, Civic Service Awards, Pilgrimages to homes of Patriots, Citizenship Forums, Representative DeMolay Contests, Founder's Trophy Contests.

Special attention is given to helping Chapters plan varied and interesting programs.

Other material sent to Chapters from time to time includes bulletins providing information for use in developing a better understanding of public problems.

Among the matters being dealt with are: Illiteracy, Poverty, International Relationships, Child Labor, Social Hygiene, Crime, Immigration, Divorce and Education.

New conditions are dealt with as they arise, affecting the social, commercial, professional and political changes constantly taking place. The object is to keep DeMolays fully informed on matters essential to their future duties as citizens.

This department has had the benefits of assistance from the following leaders: Harry H. Moore, U. S. Public Health Service, Washington; Dr. M. J. Exner of the American Social Hygiene Association, New York; Dr. John W. Brewer, Boston, Director of the Bureau of Vocational Guidance, Harvard University; Dr. Charles A. Ellwood, Professor of Sociology at the University of Missouri and 1924 President of the American Sociological Association; Frank H. Cheley, Denver, President of the Father and Son League of America; J. H. McCurdy, Springfield, Mass., Secretary of the National Physical Directors' Association; Major John L. Griffith, Chicago, Secretary of the "Big Ten" Conference and Executive Vice-President of the National Amateur Athletic Federation, and A. A. Stagg, Director of the Department of Physical Education, University of Chicago.

Department of Public Relations

George. B. Sykes.

The Order of DeMolay is the recognized leader in its field. Its wide range of activities and additions to its personnel provide innumerable news and feature stories of great interest. Newspapers and other publications will use these if they have a news value and can be depended upon to be correct. These stories may refer to members, chapters, state organizations, Grand Council, or to any person or event identified with DeMolay.

This work is handled for the Grand Scribe by a department of Public Relations. It is directed by G. B. Sykes, who has served for many years on the editorial staffs of metropolitan newspapers.

More than two thousand daily papers use news items sent out by this department. The Associated Press, United

Press, International News and other press services have been very generous in sending out stories adapted to their requirements. In addition, more than two hundred Masonic and DeMolay publications use special articles about the Order, as well as news items. Through these various channels, DeMolays and all others interested in the progress of this young mens' organization are kept posted on its activities throughout the world.

Pictures for newspapers and other publications are important factors in spreading the gospel of DeMolay. The Grand Council has a splendid collection of photographs of DeMolay drill teams, officers, athletes and of various DeMolay activities. Many have been found usable in newspapers, magazines and gravure sections. The department of Public Relations is always glad to get new pictures and also any items which may be of news interest. This department will gladly prepare articles about any phase of DeMolay desired. A request for same is all that is necessary.

The Highest Degree in DeMolay

The Legion of Honor is the highest degree awarded by the Grand Council. He who attains this distinction must be not only an outstanding DeMolay, but also active in religious and civic life of his community as well.

This service may be of the sort where all may see and appreciate; on the other hand, it may be such that is not publicly observed. The diversified activities of DeMolay chapters and the countless opportunities for usefulness found in every community, afford every member numerous ways of striving for this distinction.

Each chapter of DeMolay is entitled to recommend one member for this degree for each twenty-five candidates upon which that chapter has conferred both degrees during the fiscal year. This recommendation is made by the advisory board to the member or deputy of the Grand Council in charge of the state or district where the chapter is located. Only DeMolays who have attained the age of twenty years are eligible.

If the member or deputy is satisfied with the record of the DeMolay, he may nominate him to the Grand Council for the Legion of Honor and the final decision is made by the Grand Council at their annual meeting.

No member of a chapter or nominee should have any knowledge of a recommendation made by the advisory board. A DeMolay cannot apply for this degree.

Legion of Honor Insignia

Two distinct decorations may be worn by a DeMolay who has received the Legion of Honor.

Legion of Honor Ring.

One is a ring of gold, banded with DeMolay colors, which are separated by a thin line of gold. The banded part is broken by a Maltese Cross. The edges of the ring are beaded. On the inside of the ring is the name of the DeMolay, his Chapter and date the degree was conferred.

This ring must be worn.

The other is the medallion or emblem. It is a cross enameled in purple and gold, surmounted by a coronet. The Cross is encircled by a wreath and crossed by two swords. The words "DeMolay Legion of Honor" are engraved on the cross.

Legion of Honor Medallion or Recognition Pin.

The Representative DeMolay

The Award for All-Round Accomplishment and High Standards.

Clayton N. Watkins.

One of the earliest instincts of a fellow is to do everything better than his pals. It may be running, jumping, swimming, fighting—or even singing. This is a natural instinct and a fundamental of success. It should always be encouraged. The result is an all-round development.

With this competitive spirit as an incentive the department of Program and Activities of the Grand Council organized and launched an Annual Representative DeMolay Contest. This was in the Spring of 1924.

How Handled

Each chapter determines which of its members are best qualified to represent it. There is no limit to the number of DeMolays who may qualify from a chapter. The Advisory Council of each chapter decides that question.

Blanks for submitting an individual record of activities are sent to chapters annually by the Department of Program and Activities. It is the duty of the Advisory Council to notify chapter members and to hold a chapter contest if the DeMolays so desire. When the winner or winners have been selected the blanks, properly filled out, are sent to the Grand Council. It is from these records the final awards are made.

Three men of national reputation check over the records and determine who are Representative DeMolays. Besides the honor of winning such distinguished recognition, the winners are presented a specially designed emblem which they can forever prize.

Representative DeMolay Symbol

This emblem is the shield of the Order supported by a gold laurel wreath upholding a bar upon which is the word "Representative." At the base of the shield appears the last two numerals of the year in which the honor is won. The emblem which is presented by the Department of Program and Activities is to be worn in the coat lapel. If the DeMolay desires he can secure additional emblems from the Grand Council, have one set in a signet ring and use the other on his medallion ribbon just above the medallion.

Representative DeMolay Pin.

Some Activities Which Will Help you Win This Award

Begin now to do things which will qualify you for this high distinction. Act upon the suggestions in the following paragraphs.

Education—A good education is an important essential in life's progress. In this contest it is not a case of a high school or university training, but whether you have made an honest determined effort to acquire an education

Reading—Clean literature should be read. Topics should be diversified. A good book or magazine inspires. Trash is numbing.

Self-expression—You should have ability to think on your feet, whether it be in making a public address, talking before a small group, or to a single person. The ability to express yourself clearly and convincingly on all occasions is of great value.

Nature Interests—Get out into the fields and woods. Study the various forms of plant, animal and insect life that you will find. Get books at libraries on this subject and check up their contents with what you have discovered personally. Many surprises await you.

Life Work—It is often declared that a majority of workers are engaged in occupations unsuited to their abilities and inclinations. It is a serious mistake to try and earn a livelihood at something in which you are not interested. Failure usually results. During your DeMolay days you should begin to lay plans for your future occupation.

Health and Physical Fitness—DeMolays should know health requirements. This includes sex hygiene. Physical fitness makes you capable.

Manual Skill—A DeMolay should have some ability along mechanical or handicraft lines. He should be master of any creative talent which he possesses.

Religious Ideals—Religion gave birth to civilization. DeMolays should serve God and respect religion.

Chapter Loyalty—Attend your chapter meetings and join in its activities. There is such a wide range in these you will find something that fits your inclinations.

Citizenship—Be a good citizen in private as well as in public. Inform yourself on questions of the day and whenever possible volunteer your services in community undertakings.

Summary—These are major points considered by the judges in making awards. If you star in one but are low in others your grade will not equal the DeMolay who has a good general average.

Athletics

It would be difficult to find a young fellow who is not interested in athletics of one sort or another. Practically every young man has competitive energy in his system and athletics provide a safety valve.

DeMolay chapters that have gone in for athletics are among the liveliest in the Order. Baseball and basket ball leagues have flourished and there have been city, state and inter-state meets that have attracted wide attention.

A survey of DeMolay athletic possibilities has been made and an international program will soon be available to all chapters.

The major sports which provide the foundation for this program are baseball, basket ball, tennis, swimming, track and field events.

Through this plan there will be a big increase in the number of leagues and meets and in the development of sectional, state, inter-state, national, and eventually, international DeMolay contests. Among DeMolays are some of the greatest university, high school and other amateur athletes participating in games. Through this program, many of these young men will be afforded an opportunity to compete against each other who otherwise would not have met.

Symbolism of DeMolay Pin

The DeMolay pin is emblematic of the Order. Every design on it is of special significance and should be treasured by you. Acquaint yourself thoroughly with the meaning of each design. Learn the following by heart:

The Star is symbolic of those obligations and duties which one Brother of the Order owes to another.

The Shield is an age old emblem of protection. To DeMolays it reminds them of their duty to the weak, the defenseless and those in need of protection.

The Helmet is emblematic of that Chivalry without which there can be no true nobility of character.

The Crossed Swords denote justice, fortitude and mercy. They symbolize the unceasing warfare of DeMolays against arrogance, despotism and intolerance.

The Pearls around the border are symbols of true friendship which enriches our lives even as these jewels adorn the pin. They are ten in number and do honor to the man and nine youths whose ties of friendship drew them together in the formation of the Order.

The Crescent is a sign of secrecy constantly reminding DeMolays of their duty never to reveal the secrets of the Order or betray the confidences of a friend.

Majority Certificates

When a DeMolay reaches the age of twenty-one years, he automatically ceases to be an active member of the Order.

Members who are in good standing when they become of age are honored by their chapters with a majority service and presented with majority certificates, issued by the Grand Council. This majority service may be held as often as desired, but most chapters confer it once a year.

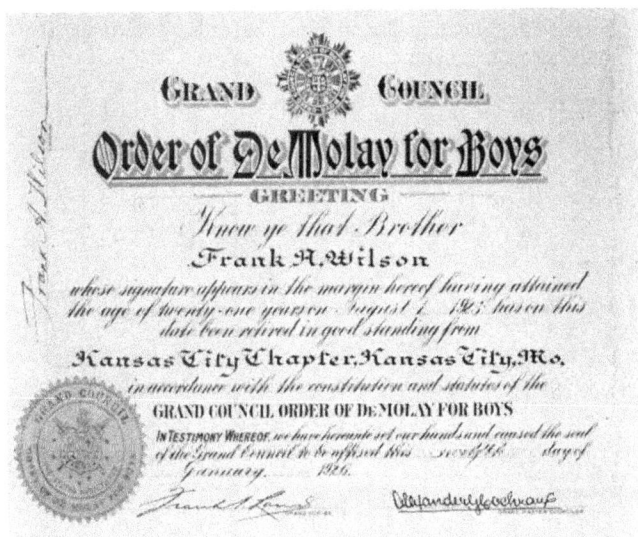

Majority Certificate.

In jurisdictions which permit visitation of chapters and activities by majority members, the majority certificate and also a yearly card, issued by the member or deputy of the Grand Council for that district, is the entrance permit. These majority members will in many cases be future advisors of chapters and their experience and counsel is of great value.

Majority certificates are ordered through the scribe of your chapter. He certifies the date when you became of age and attends to other details in the matter.

The certificate is issued under the seal of the Grand Council and has the signatures of the Grand Master Councilor and Grand Scribe. Upon it are engrossed, in old English characters the name of the member, his chapter and the date he became of age. The certificat is nine by twelve inches in size. It costs the member one dollar.

Service Certificates

DeMolays who have served faithfully as officers of chapters are entitled to a Service Certificate. This is issued by the Grand Council and must be ordered through the scribe of your chapter.

Service Certificate.

You are entitled to a certificate for each office which you have held. On each is engrossed your name, your chapter and the title and term of your office. All are signed by the Grand Master Councilor and the Grand Scribe.

DeMolays who have been Master, Senior or Junior Councilor receive certificates printed and engrossed in purple. Those for other officers are printed in red and engrossed in black.

Each certificate can be procured for one dollar. The size is nine by twelve inches, suitable for framing.

Camps for DeMolay Leaders

The Grand Council annually sponsors DeMolay camps where members of the Order get together for an exchange of ideas and experiences and discussion of problems that have a direct bearing on the progress of the Order.

A wonderful amount of good is accomplished at these camps and every DeMolay and chapter advisor who has attended has been greatly benefited. They return to their chapters with many new and progressive plans. Attendance at these camps means not only a splendid vacation but preparation for better leadership in DeMolay activities.

These camps are not run in a haphazard manner, but each day a definite program is mapped out and followed. Mornings are given over to conferences, lectures and Ritual instruction. In the afternoons, athletics and other forms of recreation prevail. At night meetings are held, following which there is a campfire or other form of entertainment.

Camp Group at Bear Lake.

Men who are leaders in their fields address those in attendance on spiritual, social, economic, educational, hygienic and governmental affairs. Chapter activities are outlined, ritual work explained and exemplified, problems of various chapters discussed and every opportunity afforded for developing leadership within the organization. Some of the leading instructors in athletics attend these camps and pass their knowledge on to the DeMolays.

Every DeMolay and chapter "Dad" who can visit one of these camps should do so. Complete information can be obtained by writing the Grand Council.

Obligatory Days

The following days are fixed as special ceremonial days and the observance of the same is made obligatory on all members of DeMolay unless prevented by unavoidable circumstances:

Day of Comfort, January 3

Did you ever stop to think what a fine thing it is to carry a little joy into the lives of others? This especially applies to those who are unfortunate— crippled children and older persons, the aged and the poor. They may be confined in hospitals or in their own homes —but they are all accessible to you. On this day take them gifts of flowers, candy, books, magazines and other friendly tokens. It will make them happy and make you feel better. Remember this day and keep it.

Devotional Day, Sunday Nearest March 18

A DeMolay loves and serves God. His daily life should reflect a reverence for religion. A Devotional Day church attendance is required of all DeMolays. When possible, chapters in a body should attend some church where special services are to be held and members actively participate in the program.

Patriots' Day, May 1

A DeMolay is a patriot every day of his life. He exemplifies his patriotism by right conduct toward his country. This day has been set set aside by the Grand Council as a time when members of the Order should express their patriotism through activities in public meetings, parades and other forms of endeavor. It is an important DeMolay day.

Educational Day
First Regular Meeting In September

Education is one of the great bulwarks of our civilization. The anchor of education is the public school. It was only a few generations ago the first public school was started.

Educational Day affords every DeMolay a chance to show his regard for the public schools and to promote general interest in this wonderful institution. This can be done by members addressing civic and other organizations, listening to talks by qualified persons and making a survey of the school situation in their district or state. This survey can encompass school buildings, equipment, sanitation, qualifications of instructors, salaries and other items pertaining to the school question. A nice feature for this day is a general chapter discussion fostering the cause of education and the public schools.

Parents Day, Sunday Preceding
November 16

Our greatest debt is to our parents. We can never express sufficient love, respect and appreciation for them, no matter how long we live. It is not always possible to openly display this love, respect and appreciation. However, Parents' Day affords members a chance to participate in special programs under the auspices of chapters wherein they can pay the homage due mothers and fathers. It is a day that should ever be observed by DeMolays.

Jacques DeMolay

This man was the last Military Grand Master of the Order of Knights Templar. He was the favorite historic hero of the nine young crusaders who started the first DeMolay chapter under "Dad" Land. They admired the courage he displayed by perishing at the stake rather than betray his fellow Knights to enemies. For this reason his name was given the new organization. Truly a fitting title to an Order that inculcates citizenship courage in young men.

H. L. Haywood of New York City, a Masonic scholar, has written a very interesting book on the life of Jacques DeMolay for the Grand Council. It can be had by sending twenty-five cents to the Grand Scribe's office. The following brief digest was gleaned from this book:

DeMolay was born in the year 1244 in Vitrey, department of Hauge Saone, France. Little is known of his early boyhood, but in 1265, when twenty-one years old, he became a member of the Order of Knights Templar. Thirty-three years later, in 1298, he was elected Grand Master.

This Order was founded about the year 1100. Its principal purpose was to protect Christianity in the Holy Land and to prevent invasion and conquest of Europe by the Turks. In its ranks were princes of royal blood and members of the finest and noblest families of Europe. It was a host with which to reckon.

Crusade followed crusade in the battle to recover the Holy Land from the infidels. The flower of European Knighthood perished in great numbers. Those were years of trial and tribulation for Christianity.

Despite the terrible sacrifice of manhood among its members, the Order amassed great wealth during the years of these crusades. This wealth aroused the covetousness of powerful enemies and ultimately resulted in its downfall.

DeMolay, as Grand Master, prepared for another crusade. He established headquarters on the Island of Cyprus in the Mediterranean, and surrounded himself with a loyal host. Leading these Knights he invaded the Holy Land, defeated the infidels or Saracens and captured Jerusalem. A wonderful victory for Christianity. The Holy Sepulchre was visited and Easter Services held on Mount Zion.

Meantime the power and wealth of the Order had aroused envy and jealousy in Phillip the Fair, King of France. Through conspiracy he placed DeMolay in his power—also many other Knights—and for seven years they were held in dungeons and tortured by most inhuman methods. Many of them died.

A decree was issued abolishing the Order of Knights Templar and perpetually prohibiting any person from joining or representing himself as a member. All Templar properties the King could find were confiscated.

Through his Commissioners the King attempted to compel DeMolay to betray the other leaders of the Order and tell where all its properties and funds could be found. Despite the rack and other tortures DeMolay refused to sacrifice his loyal adherents and was ordered burned at the stake

As the bells in the Cathedral of Notre Dame tolled the hour of seven, the night of March 18, 1314, this fearless leader was burned at the stake on a small isle in the River Seine.

Thus perished the body of DeMolay.

The body of DeMolay perished, but the soul of the man for whom the Order of DeMolay was named, will live forever.

Historical Record

Name ....

Chapter ....

Sponsored by ....

City . ...

State or Province..

Home Address ....

Date of Initiatory Degree..

Passed Initiatory Obligation Examination..........................

Date of DeMolay Degree..

Passed DeMolay Obligation Examination...........................

Medallion Number ....

Service Certificate Number...

Majority Certificate Number...

Offices I Have Held	Date Installed
....	....
....	....
....	....
....	....
....	....
....	....

Term of Office

From................................to................................

From................................to................................

From................................to................................

From................................to................................

From................................to................................

From................................to................................

Chapters Visited

Date of Visitation	Name of Chapter	City	Master Councilor

Conclaves Attended

Date	City	Presiding Officer

DeMolay Training Camps Attended

Date	Name of Camp	Location

Grand Council Honors Won

Legion of Honor...................... Date Presented..........................
Representative DeMolay........ Date Awarded..........................
Heroism Award...................... Date Presented......................

Worthy Accomplishments as a DeMolay

Date ....
....
....
....
....
....

www.ingramcontent.com/pod-product-compliance
Lightning Source LLC
Chambersburg PA
CBHW060042040426
42331CB00032B/2242